The Meaning and Purpose of Life

The Meaning and Purpose of Life

Guide and Rewards
for Living

Peter M. Kalellis

City Bear Press
Manahawkin, NJ

Cover image
Cover and book design by Lynn Else

Library of Congress Control Number: 2022939342

ISBN 978-1-7351631-6-1

Published by City Bear Press
19 Henry Drive
Manahawkin, NJ 08050
www.citybearpress.com

Printed and bound in the
United States of America

To Andy McCabe,
an admired publisher and author

Contents

Prologue

The following chapters outline twelve perspectives to assist the reader in finding meaning and purpose in one's life. They are the result of personal experience from being a psychotherapist, and a marriage and family therapist for forty-four years, plus reading and writing self-help books to help my clients. These perspectives are also heart-felt lessons that will hopefully benefit your life and pave the way to find inner peace and joy.

As you read each chapter, I encourage you to cherish any ideas that resonate with and seem important to you, and to apply them as much as possible to your life. If you find any of the ideas irrelevant, ignore them. Do exactly what you do when you eat a well-prepared fish dinner—carefully remove the bones.

Personally, this book is another effort to offer my readers comfort but also a choice or challenge to discover your own potential to enjoy your life more fully. As you read each chapter with an open heart and clear mind underline parts that you find of interest, reflect on them, and listen to the gentle whisper of your inner self, you soul.

Day after day the thoughts that surface in your mind from your reading are the seeds of perspective, passion, and hope that, in time, will grow strong. This process will help to eliminate any negativity, disappointment, or angry feelings that might interfere with your daily life.

Most of us are aware that difficult situations, suffering, and pain are inevitable parts of life. There is no escape from the realities of our fragile and vulnerable human condition. How we each face reality is the challenge that brings maturity. We may not have easy solutions to some of our problems, yet we are aware that solutions exist. We need courage and patience to identify them, but it takes effort to pursue viable solutions.

I encourage you to take opportunities to practice the lessons you learn with members of your family, friends, relatives, and trusted coworkers. Share and discuss any ideas that arise from reading this book as you may benefit others and feel rewarded with a lasting joy.

Sometimes, listening to clever advertisements and commercials that provide substitutes for happiness can lead to frustration and annoyance. We are often allured by the attraction of affluence and financial security that many people pursue. However, in our search, few ever attain true contentment. On the contrary, it precipitates an endless pursuit of material possessions that bring an external happiness but one that rarely lasts for long. This book offers readers the opportunity to find peace and lasting joy. Hopefully, this book and the messages contained in each of the fifteen perspective—one per chapter—will help you stay on a straight path and become your friendly guide.

1

"Thy Will Be Done"

Have you ever asked the question: *Why Are We Here?* It took me some years. I was simply excited to be alive and felt eager to grow up, become an adult—free and independent—and have a good and rewarding life. We are aware and know that we were conceived when one of our father's multi-thousand sperm met one of our mother's unique ova. We do not exactly know how it happened, but we do know that life was conceived and provided loving care for the next nine months— room service for our growth in our mother's womb.

Finally, a baby boy or girl emerged from the mother's birth canal. She experienced labor pains, but when she saw the child's face probably became excited, smiled, and felt instant relief and joy that would last for many years.

Like any healthy newborn child, we kept growing faster in the first few months than at any other time. During this early stage, we also developed bonds of love and trust with our mother. We could hear her voice as she uttered soothing words and phrases to us or sang songs that we could not yet understand. It was her voice that we liked to hear. Like any good and loving parent, she tried to make us feel comfortable and content.

The character of each human being is formed and shaped in the first ten years. According to one's lifestyle and parents, each family strives to raise a normal child. During this period, the parents have hopefully instilled in their fast-growing child some reasonable and positive programming.

During the teenage years, children go through many changes—physical, hormonal, emotional, mental, and spiritual. Parents face various issues, as they notice that their son or daughter suddenly becomes independent in making their own decisions. Preventing such initiatives tends to prove counterproductive.

As a psychotherapist, my suggestion for these concerned parents during these formative years is to pull back, be patient, and observe the growth of your son or your daughter with love. In view of your good intentions and the positive foundation you have developed as parents, think about what is important. Obviously, as mature parents you want to raise healthy, normal, and happy children. Avoid preaching, criticizing, judging, or even punishing.

Parents often ask, "But what if they make terrible mistakes?" Remember that mistakes often leave behind meaningful lessons.

Now, leaving these developmental years behind can vary from culture to culture and from family to family. Let's deal with what is important and do justice to the question: Why are we here?

Often, when we are facing difficult times, we ask such questions about our purpose for living or what is the meaning of our life. When we experience serious illness or fail in one of our plans or when we are confronted with the fear of death, it is human and natural to ponder our purpose in life. Even when we feel that we are blessed abundantly we may still feel and wonder why we are feeling unhappy. Despite the abundance of many good things we enjoy in life, we may still be looking for something else, something deeper, without really knowing what that could be.

This search becomes even more puzzling when we may have had success and accomplished much in life. It is both my professional and personal experience that without a good relationship with God, our life seems to lack true meaning and purpose. You may ask, "Why is this the case?" It is usually because our life is based on what we *want* to do, instead of how we are responding to God's will. What do we mean by: *"Thy will be done,"* when we recite the Lord's Prayer? A similar phrase or intention is found in various religious or spiritual traditions that encourage the followers to develop a strong relationship with God. To be fully alive and truly happy in our personal lives, we must have a good relationship with God, our Creator. Such a relationship not only opens the possibility of a good and rewarding life, but it may also help us to be supportive of others.

A major part of our purpose in life is feeling grateful for what God has done for us. God gave us and continues to give us life. He cares for us just as good parents care for a child. What a great feeling to believe and to know that we are sons and daughters of a loving God. He came to us in human form as Jesus Christ and spoke to us about his love, his unconditional acceptance of us, and his forgiveness.

Throughout his earthly mission, Jesus showed his love and compassion for sinners. He restored the sick to health, gave sight to the blind, healed the paralytic, fed the hungry and the poor, and brought back to life those who had died.

Jesus called his disciples to follow him and to learn from him. The disciples discovered their purpose in life when Jesus entered their lives. He called them from their former vocations and gave them the purpose of being fishers of men, ambassadors of love, forgiveness, and reconciliation. He sent the disciples out and gave them a purpose for living—to proclaim the kingdom of God—God's love and forgiveness.

The apostle Paul was a fanatic Jew who persecuted Christians and sought to destroy the Church. He thought this was his purpose in life. But when he met Jesus on the road to Damascus, he discovered his true purpose. He was called to spread the gospel of God's love to people who had never heard it before. God also calls us and gives purpose and meaning to our lives.

In having a good relationship with our Creator and his overwhelming and steadfast love, we discover our purpose. We are called to love God and to be of service to his people. Jesus came "not to be served but to serve" (Matt 20:28). What a blessing it is to help others in need.

❦ ❦

For Reflection

When you consider your life at this moment, what makes you truly alive and happy?

2

Self-Acceptance

This chapter is about accepting your true self, that is, loving and respecting your life, and cherishing your own capabilities, talents, and the gifts that God has given you. Look deeper into yourself for you will be happier when you learn to accept who you are.

Self-acceptance is important. Try not to be hard on yourself and judgmental about your thoughts, feelings, and beliefs. It is important sometimes to let things be as they are, and to allow yourself to breathe without questioning or trying to fix the problems that confront you. If necessary, make a list of your current concerns and consider ways that you can work toward confronting those concerns. Include how you feel and what reasonable actions might be used to combat your concerns.

Once you begin to believe and feel that you are in good standing with God and that you have a good relationship with our Lord Jesus, you will feel more confident in who you are. We are happier knowing that God, our loving Creator, has accepted us and loves us as sons and daughters unconditionally. Consequently, we gratefully return to our self and learn to accept who we truly are. When we look deeper into our hearts, we become aware of our human condition. Strengths and weaknesses may surface, but it is our choice to make characteristic changes.

Self-acceptance is a spiritual concept and practice. It may be a powerful answer to our relationships, regardless of whether we are single, married, or in a relationship. It has been a powerful tool for me and for my clients who seek personal therapy. The type of acceptance I am referring to is not about giving up, nor is it about shutting down our frustration and fear. It is more spiritual, the acceptance that comes from meditation and prayer. Such acceptance brings peace. It is to understand that if the thing we want the most is not meant to be in our present life, then we pray and hope that there is something better, or something more purposeful for us in our Lord's time.

Patience, persistence, and prayer are three important tools that we can all apply. We have no other reliable source except to turn to our loving God who accepts us, knows us, and loves us unconditionally. Our choice is to accept who we truly are. When we do this, it becomes easier to accept others.

As we communicate with God and focus on our requests, we might experience a connection, a feeling of inner joy, and a closeness to our Lord Jesus. Truly, our parents bring us into the world, but it is God who gives us life and sustains us with caring love.

Human beings are created after the image of God. We are also spiritual beings, carrying within our physical body a particle of God, our soul. Sometimes, our soul is disturbed by events in our life and may get tarnished by negative, external forces. But our Lord Jesus Christ always forgives us and invites us to rediscover and restore our unique personal self-image.

Self-acceptance is crucial to our daily existence. If we accept ourselves, we become free to live life to its fullest. If we are negative about who we are and cannot accept ourselves, then we deprive ourselves of vitality and inner peace. We experience an inner serenity only when we walk in the Lord's presence. As St. Paul told the Athenians and reminds us, it is "in him we live and move and have our being" (Acts 17:28) that we discover the priceless steps in becoming more like Christ.

Our thoughts are an important part of giving us life and how we can manage them to improve and refine our daily existence. Personally, as I have explored life's complexities, especially obstacles to a healthier lifestyle, I have concluded that it is ultimately my responsibility to identify these obstacles and do my best to resolve them, or at least find ways to use them to rise higher spiritually.

Resolution implies discipline, a gradual process of identifying and rooting out destructive patterns of behavior, negative thinking, destructive behavior and carefully replacing them with new, constructive and positive attitudes. To regain and sustain a healthier self involves developing resources that facilitate and nurture this process of restoration.

With care and sensitivity, we need to ask ourselves what it is that we want from life. What steps do we need to take to attain a reasonably satisfying existence? Patiently, we allow time to hear the answer from within—a whisper from the heart.

Self-acceptance means to receive willingly and to accept completely our true self. No joy can be fostered without self-acceptance; no growth can occur; and no human relationship can sustain itself without it. Self-acceptance helps us to modify our behavior.

By accepting our self, we may feel a strong urge to change, not because there is something wrong with us, but because our soul, our inner self, knows that there is more to life to enjoy.

Sometimes we may wish to change a behavior or attitude that has served us in the past, but we realize that these efforts no longer serve a purpose; they may even hurt us. So, why hold on to them? At times, our inner demons will fog our mind and tell us that we are weak and worthless, and that death is our destiny. We must be aware of such demons: one may be the attraction to be successful; another may be the compulsion to be right; and yet another may be the desire to be powerful and in control.

You and I may wrestle with these alluring demons, but we don't need to join them, for their intention is to deprive us of the truth and prevent us from being happy. Self-acceptance is the full realization that we are not God; we are human. Our part is to become aware that we are all right just the way we are because we are created by God. Any corrections and improvements can only be done in the spirit of humility and gentleness. As we feel and apply compassion for others, it is essential to remember that we are one with them.

We must be strong, confident, and accepting of our self before accepting others. So, let's forgive ourselves and free ourselves from feeling guilty, inadequate, or responsible, and celebrate being human.

Combat our demons and any negative influences is an ongoing process of patience, perseverance, and prayer. Patiently approach life by seeking out people and situations that may be nurturing and by doing things that you love doing.

Warm your heart with love and reach out to give love to others. You may be surprised when you rediscover your own capacity to love. Take a few minutes each day and start loving those who are close to you— your family, your friends, and your colleagues. Many of them may be soothed and healed by the tenderness of your love. When you return to your inner self, reflect on every move that you have made and whether it has been in accordance with God's will.

❧ ❧

For Reflection

What real actions can you take to grow in accepting your true Self unconditionally?

3

Self-Care

M any healing professionals agree that the people who are often more satisfied, fulfilled, and happy are those who are eager to begin the day, who exercise, take a shower, have breakfast, and who feel that they have something to contribute. Having discussed and reflected on self-acceptance, the true person, in the previous chapter, we can now consider self-care.

Self-care does not mean looking in a mirror and only seeing yourself and nobody else. It does not justify an attitude of *me, myself, and I.* It means accepting, loving, and respecting yourself. No one can be like anybody else. You can only be who you are and that's okay. You are a son or a daughter of a loving God.

We are not God. We are humans with potentials to make our life rewarding, but we cannot be the center of the universe. When we are successful and have great accomplishments but ignore God as the giver of all life's blessings, we set ourselves up for disappointment and frustration. Our pride or false ego is never satisfied and is always thirsting for more. It is better, however, to embrace our moments of success and accomplishments as an opportunity to thank God for our life and for God's unconditional love for us.

It is important to care for your body, mind, and soul every day. Our body is God's gift to each of us. So, we need to befriend our body and stop being judgmental of some mistake that we may have made. Diligent self-care will keep you healthy, fit, resilient, and happy. However, practicing self-care isn't always easy.

Many of us tend to be very busy with stressful jobs and families to support. Some people are overconsumed with evolving technology to make time for themselves. Stress generally refers to two things: the pressure of psychological perception and the body's response to it. Such stress can have multiple results ranging from digestion to metabolism to muscle tightness and memory loss.

So, how does one engage in self-care? First, it is advisable to find a self-care strategy that is especially helpful for you. Ask your doctor, read an article, or choose an activity that brings you some benefit. Anything good in life requires some effort. Regardless of the approach you take, it is important to take good care of your body, mind, and soul each day.

When you take some time out, specifically to rest, relax, or have fun, try not to feel guilty or that you are being selfish. As you feel good physically, mentally, and spiritually, you will find it most rewarding to reach out and help someone who may need help. The following ten ideas may be helpful in developing your self-care strategy.

1. *Be organized.* Being organized requires discipline. It is often the first step in taking care of yourself. A major issue is to take a peripheral glance around your immediate environment and see if there is any clatter—objects and gadgets that you no longer use—and get rid of them because they consume your energy. Use a notebook to write down things you need to buy or do, such as your tasks and appointments. You may also create an area to store briefcases, your coats, keys, backpacks, and make sure they're ready to go for the next day.

2. *Eat healthy meals.* If you drive a car, you use the right kind of fuel and make sure the oil is regularly changed. Like your

car, your body needs nourishing meals. Many people don't take time to prepare themselves a nourishing meal, preferring instead to stop at a fast-food restaurant or heating up a frozen meal in the microwave. Unfortunately, these "fast" meals usually aren't sufficient to provide your body with the right calories and nutrients. Even if it's only once a week, consider making a healthy meal for yourself and your family.

3. *Exercise regularly.* Start taking a regular walk. For the first week, for starters, walk moderately for ten to fifteen minutes. In the second week, walk a bit more firmly for twenty minutes, and during the third week, walk for thirty to thirty-five minutes. By the end of the month, you will realize the momentum that you have gained. You will feel better and walking will become a positive and beneficial step in taking good care of yourself. You may decide to go to a gym where professionals will help you to improve your physical health.

4. *Develop a sleep routine.* Now in my 90s and suffering from a lack of regular sleep has

caused health issues. I'm grateful to good physicians who have helped improve my sleep routine. Eating or drinking before going to bed can disturb your sleep. It's especially important to stay away from caffeine, Coca-Cola, refreshments, and eating sweets that may cause sleeplessness. Make sure that your bedroom is conducive to getting a good night's rest. The quality of sleep affects your health as much as the length of sleep. Try to be free of distractions, such as shows on television, a laptop, or your cellphone. Make sure you have a comfortable bed with a firm mattress, so you don't wake up in the morning with back aches and pains.

5. *Read.* Americans have made entertainment a major part of their life. Mass media, social media, television, and the internet have raised the standard of entertainment but has also deprived the public of educational or psycho-spiritual books to read. In today's fast-paced world, we tend to turn to our phones for entertainment or comfort. Scrolling through the latest news can contribute to stress and anxiety rather than ease it. Reading a book can

sometimes make a difference and slow you down instead of constantly checking your phone for messages. Reading can help to improve your mood, but it can also help you to stay more present, mindful, and appreciative of your present life.

6. *Learn to say no.* Learning to say no can be challenging. Many of us feel obligated to say yes when someone asks for a favor that takes effort, time, and energy. If you're already stressed or overworked, saying yes to loved ones or colleagues can lead to burnout, anxiety, and irritability. It may take some practice, but once you learn how to say no politely, you will feel more empowered and have more time to care for yourself.

7. *Take a self-care trip.* Taking a self-care trip can make a huge difference to your life. Even if you're not feeling particularly stressed, getting away for a weekend occasionally can help you to disconnect from a taxing agenda, relax, and be rejuvenated. Self-care trips don't need to be costly. The goal is to get away from your normal schedule and take time to do something just for yourself.

8. *Get outside.* Spending time outside and exploring the glory of nature can help reduce stress, lower your blood pressure, and increase mindfulness. Studies have shown that getting outside can reduce fatigue and help overcome symptoms of burnout or depression. Getting outside can also help you sleep better at night, especially if physical activity, like hiking or walking, are involved.

9. *Adopt a pet.* Pets can be hugely beneficial for our self-care. They can give us unconditional love and provide companionship. Dogs especially can help reduce stress and feelings of anxiety and even lower our blood pressure. In fact, many people who suffer from disorders like posttraumatic stress disorder have benefited from working daily with animals.

10. *Respect and love yourself.* Schedule and guard your time for self-care. It can be difficult to find extra time, but it's extremely important to plan regular self-care time. These self-care moments will help you to ponder the best ways to move forward in your life and keep you grounded just like moments with friends can help you feel

more connected and relaxed. Look for small ways you can incorporate such time into your everyday life. For example, you might wake up fifteen minutes earlier and practice deep breathing before the chaos of the day begins, or you might take a walk around the block after your breakfast or lunch. The more you can work self-care time into your schedule, the better you'll be able to relax, grow spiritually, enjoy your life, and thrive.

It is important to care for your wellness otherwise you will have to deal with illness. As you leave behind some of the noises and chaos of your life, your mind will clear, and you will regain inner peace. It is your decision to save the only life you can save, your own which is God's gift.

೫ ೯

For Reflection

What self-care strategy can you develop in your life that will make a difference to you physically, mentally, and spiritually?

4

Self-Examination

More than two thousand years ago, Socrates said that "an unexamined life is not worth living." I have often wondered what this profound axiom means.

In re-examining my life, I realized that the person whom I often presented to my friends and to society was not my true self but rather the one whom I thought would be pleasing to others—polite, confident, successful, and happy—so that I would be liked and admired. However, it is the true self that is approved and desired by God. Feeling accepted and validated by God, I recalled the psalm: *"O Lord, you have searched me and known me. You know when I sit down and when I rise up; you discern my thoughts from far away....For it was you who formed my inward parts; you knit me together in my mother's womb. I praise you, for I am fearfully and wonderfully made"* (Psalm 139:1–2; 13–14).

Examining your life begins with who you are at this moment and respecting yourself as God's creation. You don't have to be severely critical or judgmental when examining your life for God is love. He is the only judge. Remember that God loves you as a parent loves a child and often more for the parts of the child that are weaker or where the child struggles and falters. Often, it is our very weaknesses that remind us that we can rely fully on God's grace. St. Paul reassures us: "I will boast all the more gladly of my weaknesses, so that the power of Christ may dwell in me. Therefore I am content with weaknesses, insults, hardships, persecutions, and calamities for the sake of Christ; for whenever I am weak, then I am strong" (2 Cor 12:9–10).

Our belief that everyone is called to be a daughter or son of God has profound implications for our daily life. It is this loving acceptance that can imbue even the quietest moments of one's life with grace. The invitation to be God's adopted children continually draws us closer to God, who wants nothing more than to transform us.

It is important to ask how we, as human beings, can have a genuine relationship with our Creator. We all face adversities, problems that we did not expect and that do not have easy solutions. Many people are hurting physically or mentally. As we grow, we experience external influences that can be negative. We feel burdened by our anxieties and fears, but comfort comes as we reach out and connect with our Lord Jesus Christ through prayer. With Christ's help, we overcome major fears and difficulties in life, including the greatest one of all, the fear of death.

As we grow and mature, our worldview develops from our many experiences and relationships. Today, there are clearly two worldviews: one, a *secular* worldview, which claims that human beings are the central focus of our life and events; another, a *Christian* worldview, which believes that God is the sovereign and active power in our everyday life.

A secularist, on the one hand, believes that a human being is basically good, in charge of his or her own fate by making decisions to pursue success and attain knowledge. Moral standards for the secularist are unconstrained, and humans are entitled to choose by their own direction.

A Christian, on the other hand, believes that an all-powerful God has created the heavens and the earth. This living and omnipotent God possesses all knowledge, and because of God's great love for humanity, he has established absolute moral standards for our protection. God is holy, loving, and personal.

Through the Incarnation, God, in human form, has bridged the gap between God and the world, opening the way for each one of us. God, our Creator, put on humanity so that we might put on divinity. In becoming human, God empowered us to share God's own divine nature. With God in our hearts, we can do what is important and needs to be done for our spiritual benefit.

As we visualize Christ's appearance and life on earth, how he touched and healed people, we sense the ceaseless pulse of divine love as it nurtures our hearts. The personality of Jesus Christ is a good model for us. While we cannot be Christ, as we follow his exemplary life, we discover our true self, who we really are. We have a chance to participate in the work of the Holy Spirit whose purpose is to refine us and to make us temples of God's presence. As St. Paul reminds us, "Do not be conformed to this world, but be transformed by the renewing of your minds, so that you may discern what is the will of God" (Rom 12:2).

As we become more aware of our human condition, we may want to change certain aspects that are undesirable. The power of prayer is remarkable. It is a firm ladder which joins earth to heaven. It is through prayer that we become closer to God whose energies will become more available to us. It is through consistent prayer, that we can become enlightened, sinners can become saints, and we can experience an inner serenity as we walk in the Lord's presence and become more like Christ. Furthermore, through prayer and experiencing God in our life, we gain strength to overcome certain obstacles, and we can develop healthier relationships with others. We see others as God sees them, as sons and daughters, members of God's kingdom.

As we interweave Christian virtues into our relationships, we sense God's creative energy within. What are those virtues? We act on our Lord's behalf, emulating his spirit and applying his virtues of compassion, forgiveness, justice, love, and total acceptance. For example:

- We can accept and love those who are not returning love to us.
- We find joy and inner peace even in difficult times.
- We show patience when things are not going as we expected.
- We show kindness toward those who treat us unkindly.
- We find inner strength to fight temptation.

Personally, my self-growth and spiritual awakening were entirely dependent on being aware that I was not just a physical body. I also had an inner active engine, an invisible part within me, a soul that kept my body functioning and alive.

My daily self-examination involves asking questions pertinent to my self-image. For example, as I was going through personal therapy, there was a time I pondered how my parents had wounded me, especially my stepmother and other adults. Later, as a therapist, listening to other people's problems, I realized how they too have experienced hurts by parents, partners, spouses, relatives, or friends.

Life's hurts may leave scars, but fortunately they are reminders of the human potential for survival. Eventually, I arrived at a comforting thought that people who had hurt us were most likely hurt by others. Each of us, as well as those who have gone before us, share the human condition, and suffer from imperfect love. My challenge as a therapist has been that, while I may not be able to stop the emotional pain of my hurts or heal my wounds totally, I can at least attend to my spiritual thirst for healing. Furthermore, while I may not be able to regain the love that I missed from significant others, like my parents, our loving God and Lord Jesus Christ provides perfect love. It is a timely reminder that I am created after the *image* and *likeness* of God (cf. Gen 1:26)—being created in the *image* of God implies that I am a *spiritual* being; being created in God's *likeness* implies that, like God, I am a creative being.

That humans are created after the image of God distinguishes us from the animals and other creatures.

However, being created in God's likeness brings with it our awesome responsibility of exercising stewardship and participating with God in managing the vastness of God's creation. Our human body is a likeness of God, designed to reveal insights into the church, the "body of Christ" assisting capable people to continue God's work on earth.

Dr. Ellsworth Wareham, a humble yet brilliant cardiac surgeon who volunteered and devoted his life to patients who needed surgery in less developed countries, is an example of the likeness of God, living the kind of Christian life that exemplified what is portrayed in the Book of Genesis.

Georgia Christopher, a widow and active member of the Holy Trinity Church in Westfield, New Jersey, is gifted in interior decorating. She, along with two other women, converted a simple four-wall auditorium into a church. Georgia also generously donated large sums of money for a mission to Africa, allowing the Christian missionary work to continue.

Knowing these two kindhearted people well, I believe their love for Christ was not in words but alive in action. Their contribution came from their hearts— caring, loving, and acting.

By examining and re-examining my life, I discovered the importance of a genuine relationship with Jesus who loves me unconditionally. His love has helped me to accept my true self. Examining my life has helped me to continue my inner journey and look forward to my return to the safety of my faith that has brought me an awareness of God's presence within me. As you gently examine your own life my you also find God's presence within.

❦ ❦

For Reflection

As you examine your own life, are there moments when Christ has been a model for your actions? Have there been other people in your life who have been Christ-like?

5

Facing Life's Adversities

To know our inner self is to learn who God is and the steps that we must take to make our existence more rewarding.

Gradually, we become aware and learn that our lifestyle's motivations—our values, dreams, goals, and beliefs are not what we have been told by others, but rather, what we have discovered ourselves. Ultimately, we believe that God cares and has a plan for each of us. God gives us power and wisdom to face the adversities throughout our life.

St. Peter offers steps to strengthen our spiritual life. He advocates several attitudes that are essential if we are to respond wisely in times of illness and suffering and reminds us of our Christian discipleship:

You are a chosen race, a royal priesthood, a holy nation, God's own people, in order that you may proclaim the mighty acts of him who called you out of darkness into his marvelous light....

And all of you must clothe yourselves with humility in your dealings with one another for "God opposes the proud, but gives grace to the humble." Humble yourselves therefore under the mighty hand of God, so that he may exalt you in due time. Cast all your anxiety on him, because he cares for you. (1 Pet 2:9; 5:5–7)

For a believer, there is never any occasion that warrants any other attitude than Christ-like humility and self-discipline. Elsewhere, St. Peter states: "Always be ready to make your defense to anyone who demands from you an accounting for the hope that is in you; yet do it with gentleness and reverence" (1 Pet 3:15).

Pain and suffering can take many different forms and effects. The Bible doesn't trivialize our experience of suffering by saying that it's all a storm and will subside or pass away sooner than one may think. Rather, it recognizes the different forms of adversity. St. Paul notes, "We are afflicted in every way, but not crushed; perplexed, but not driven to despair; persecuted, but not forsaken; struck down, but not destroyed" (2 Cor 4:8–9). And in the Book of Revelation, it states:

> And I heard a loud voice from the throne saying,
>
> "See, the home of God is among mortals.
> He will dwell with them;
> they will be his peoples,
> and God himself will be with them;
> he will wipe every tear from their eyes.
> Death will be no more;
> mourning and crying and pain will be
>   no more,
> for the first things have passed away."
>   (Rev 21:3–4)

So our suffering is not random or without purpose.

The church is to be a refuge for those who are going through difficult times, a hospital for the wounded hearts. When a member is hurting, the church applies the bandages; when a member is down, the church encourages and extends a hand of support; when a member is in need, the church comes alongside to help. St. Paul confirms this when he writes, "Bear one another's burdens, and in this way you will fulfill the law of Christ" (Gal 6:2).

St. John Chrysostom, an early church father of the fourth century, writes that the church is like a clinic. Throughout the week, people face different problems, they get hurt, they feel wounded, so they come to church, the spiritual clinic for comfort and healing that is available by the loving grace of our Lord Jesus Christ, the physician of bodies and souls.

When we have passed through our own trials and tribulations, we will experience the presence of Jesus Christ. Adversities are part of human existence from birth until death, and every person goes through illness or pain: physically, mentally, socially, or spiritually. Such adversities are an inescapable feature of human existence.

You may ask: "Why do I suffer? Why do others suffer? How can suffering be overcome? Is there any meaning to suffering?" To understand the "whys" of suffering, we must look to our Lord's divine love. He is the ultimate source for understanding the meaning and purpose of everything that exists.

The mission of the only begotten Son of God consists in conquering sin and overcoming death by his cross and resurrection. During his life, Christ restored sight to the blind, healed the sick and cured the lepers, gave food to the hungry, and brought the dead to life. Christ may not answer our human questioning about life's adversities or the meaning of suffering directly.

But he invites us to follow him and to take part in his work of saving our own soul and helping others.

Salvation, inner peace, and joy are attained through Christ's suffering, through his cross. When an individual takes up his cross, he or she is spiritually united to the cross of Christ, as St. Paul reminds all Christians, "As many of you as were baptized into Christ have clothed yourselves with Christ" (Gal 3:27).

In reflecting on St. Paul's message, being clothed with Christ means that I'm never alone. Christ is always with me. And when he is with me, who or what can be against me? In taking this journey—reflecting and writing about it—I am aware that I'm not travelling alone, regardless of how long my travel is each hour of the day. Sometimes, the journey is tedious; other times, it is full of adventure and excitement, offering uncommon experiences and potentially more knowledge. I do not foresee much trouble on the way unless my soul is troubled by recounting the unhappy or even painful events of my past. Being sensitive, I try not to keep thinking about the past. I also try not to be in a hurry to arrive at some immediate goal. It is better if my journey lasts for a long time. Periodically, it is good to stop on the way and meet people and learn from their experiences. As I move closer to a century, I am feeling healthy, happy, fully alive, and creative. The issue of aging is God's dominion, and I'm grateful.

For Reflection

What are some of the ways that you experience pain and suffering in your life? How does your faith help you to overcome these feelings?

6

Why Are We Tested?

This question reminds me of Jesus and how he was tested during his forty days in the desert. Whether we believe Satan appeared in some physical way to test Jesus personally or whether Jesus experienced these tests or temptations within himself, we really don't know.

The temptations in the desert may be the easiest part of Jesus's life to understand. We are all subjected to being tested. While writing this chapter, a client had come to my office for therapy. I remembered her as a client eighteen years ago, but this time she was very emotional. When she stopped crying, she wiped her tears and sat across from me in silence.

Knowing that she was married with two sons, I asked, "Dorothy, what is the problem?"

"I feel frustrated and very angry," she said, eyes still brimming with tears.

"Last night over an argument, my husband suggested that we get a divorce. I could not believe my ears. After thirty-five years of being together and having two teenage sons, he is thinking of a divorce."

"What caused the argument?" I asked.

"Something stupid."

"Something stupid and you are so upset? Could there be something else?" I asked speculating that Dorothy had been tested.

"There are many things. All my married life, I have tried to please him, to make him happy by keeping our house clean, doing the laundry, caring for his shirts, shopping for groceries, making good meals for the family, but recently I do not feel appreciated. I feel ignored! He no longer brings me flowers or takes me out to some occasional dinner in a special restaurant." She paused and sighed, "There's no more romance. My heart is aching, and I don't think he cares."

"Can you think of anything good about your husband?" I asked.

"Well, he works very hard and financially we are doing well. He never complains when I spend money on the kids or on myself."

"Dorothy, your emotional pain and anger need to be dealt with," I said. "Let me suggest that next time you make an appointment, you and your husband come to my office together. I do not perform miracles, but doing marriage counseling for many years, I believe you could use some good professional help, at least to regain peace of mind and make some adjustments in your married life."

As she opened the door to leave, she paused and asked, "Doctor, next time can I come alone, just by myself? I need to be more honest with you and share another part of myself."

"You can come alone," I said.

Pausing for few seconds, she said. "I'm not as good as I think I am. I'm angry at God and the world around me for not being satisfied for the good things that I have." And pursing her lips she blubbered, "I'm irritable, and I find some stupid reasons to scream at my husband and turn my misery on him."

"I'll see you alone next time," I said, being empathetic. Sensing Dorothy's pain, she was another person on my list of clients who were being tested in their life and were suffering mentally, spiritually, and physically.

In both the Old and the New Testaments, the verb "to test" is translated as "to prove by trial." Therefore, when God tests us, we believe that it is to prove that our faith is real. Now, it is not that God needs to prove it, since God already knows all things, but God wants to reassure us that our faith is real.

Sometimes, God tests our faith, just as God tested the faith of the ancient Israelites by allowing them to go through hard times in the desert, "in order to make known to them what was in their hearts" (cf. Deut 8:2). God knows our strengths and weakness. If our faith is weak, it may not be obvious when our life is satisfactory and going smoothly. But when hard times come, a weak faith will be evident for what it really is—shallow and unable to help us through life's difficulties.

The test may be an unexpected illness, a costly accident, the death of a loved one, the loss of a job, or a friend who turns against us. When hard times happen, we discover the true nature of our faith. God may test us so that we can realize our potential and strength. Now, none of us likes to go through hard times and God isn't necessarily behind these hard times.

But God does sometimes allow us to experience hard times. The Book of Genesis tells us how God tested Abraham, asking him to take his knife and sacrifice his only son, Isaac: "When they came to the place that God had shown him, Abraham built an altar there and laid the wood in order. He bound his son, Isaac, and laid him on the altar, on top of the wood. Then Abraham reached out his hand and took the knife to kill his son. But the angel of the Lord called to him from heaven, and said, "Abraham, Abraham!" And he said, "Here I am." He said, "Do not lay your hand on the boy or do anything to him; for now I know that you fear God, since you have not withheld your son, your only son, from me" (Gen 22:9–12).

Here we see how God tests Abraham whose faith in God leaves with us a serious lesson. God may use or allow some adversity to show us our human strengths or weaknesses. And should this happen, we need to ask God to increase our faith. Through testing we are made spiritually stronger the more we believe in God.

King David sought God's testing, asking him to examine his heart and mind and see if they were true to him (cf. Psalm 26:2; 139:23). In Job, we have an example of God allowing one of his faithful people to be tested by the devil. Job bore all his trials patiently and "did not sin or charge God with wrongdoing" (Job 1:22). However, the account of Job's testing is proof that Satan's ability to try us is limited by God's sovereign control. All our trials work toward God's perfect purpose and for our benefit.

In the New Testament, St. James writes: "My brothers and sisters, whenever you face trials of any kind, consider it nothing but joy, because you know that the testing of your faith produces endurance; and let endurance have its full effect, so that you may be mature and complete, lacking in nothing" (Jas 1:1–4). James goes on to say that testing is a blessing, because, when the testing is over and we have "stood the test," we will "receive the crown of life that God has promised to those who love him" (v. 12).

Testing comes from our heavenly Father who works all things together for good for those who love him and who are called to be the children of God (cf. Rom 8:28).

The various biblical examples of being tested remind us of the words of Philaret, a spiritual Russian monk that I have used as part of my prayers for many years:

> In every hour of the day, reveal Your will to me. Bless my dealings with all who surround me. When I feel tested, I pray for strength. Dear Lord Jesus, please teach me to treat all that comes to me throughout the day with peace of soul, clarity of mind and with the firm conviction that Your will governs all. In all my deeds and words, guide my thoughts and feelings. In unforeseen events, let me not forget that all are sent by You. Teach me to act firmly and wisely, without embittering and embarrassing others.
>
> Give me strength to bear the fatigue of the coming day with patience. In any hour of the day, reveal Your will to me. Bless my dealings with all who surround me. Teach me

to treat any test that I face throughout the day with peace of soul, clarity of mind and with the firm conviction that you are a God of love who is in charge of His children. In all my deeds and words, guide my thoughts, feelings, and actions. In unforeseen events, let me not forget that all are sent by You. Teach me to act firmly and wisely, without embittering and embarrassing others. Give me strength to bear the fatigue of the coming day with all that it shall bring. Direct my will; teach me to pray, pray Yourself in me, Lord Jesus. Amen.

To be true Christians often requires us to move out of our comfort zone and into the unknown. Our testing or trials come in various forms. Yet perseverance in testing results in spiritual maturity and completeness.

When we experience the storms of life, we should be like the tree that digs its roots ever more deeply for a greater grip in the earth. We must dig our roots more deeply into God's grace and cling to God's promises so that we can weather whatever storms come against us. As St. Paul writes of the Lord, "My grace is sufficient for you, for power is made perfect in weakness" and he reminds us, "Therefore I am content with weaknesses, insults, hardships, persecutions, and calamities for the sake of Christ; for whenever I am weak, then I am strong" (2 Cor 12:9–10).

God is reaching out to all of us. In any test or trial that you endure, hear what God says, "I will never leave you or forsake you" (Heb 13:5). That is God's promise to you. God sticks with us, even when we are at our worst—that's grace which comes in the name of Jesus Christ.

❧ ❧

For Reflection

When you consider the many ways that you are tested in your life, how can these sometimes-painful moments be opportunities for growth?

7

Pain and Suffering

If we are suffering due to chronic pain, it is recommended that we seek professional help from a doctor who can relieve the physical pain. If we are suffering from emotional problems, it may be advisable to seek professional help from a psychotherapist. When people fail to seek professional help, they invite inevitable pain that can result in chronic suffering. Both pain and suffering can be preventable by seeking the right help, whatever that may be, at the right time.

Continuous suffering can be a very different problem, brought on by serious losses and despairs and the overwhelming awareness that in this life, we always exist in the space between the imagined ideal and the reality of life. This tension enables us to reach our highest creative potential and to realize who we really are as humans. During emotional torment, we can become more open to new directions. In other words, suffering can expand our human potential.

As a psychotherapist for more than four decades, I have had the opportunity to see people who were undergoing a different kind of unbearable emotional or physical pain. To be of some comfort, I can say that I have experienced my own human vulnerability. I may not feel someone's pain and be able to wipe away tears to bring comfort, but I can certainly empathize with their agony.

Recently, a couple confirmed for me that one of their most painful experiences resulting in intense suffering was the loss of their 34-year-old son. Jerry and Cathy, a couple in their early sixties experienced the most devastating pain a parent can face when their younger son was killed in a car accident. The child's image and memory will forever remain vividly in a parent's heart. The age of the child at the time of death does not lessen the hurt or devastation. It feels completely unnatural for a child to die before his or her parents.

Many grieving parents question whether life will hold any more meaning for them and how they will survive the pain of their loss. Some parents describe the feeling as having *a wound in their heart* that will never heal; others blame themselves and believe that God is punishing them for some reason, or regret that they did not spend more time with their child when he or she was alive. Others may become angry with society and what they see as a hostile world, or they may blame the physician for misdiagnosing their child's illness.

Even though more than fifty thousand children under the age of 21 die every year in the United States, it does not ease the pain of their loss. Such feelings of anger, sadness, confusion, depression, irritability, low self-esteem, and emptiness do not mean that you are losing your mind or becoming crazy or insane. If you are experiencing emotional pain while mourning the loss of a child, such thoughts and feelings are normal.

There is a theory that human suffering is the gateway through which we must pass so as to develop our higher faculties. I'm still looking for meaning in this theory. Perhaps the true revelations can be found in the wisdom of those who experienced direct and merciless suffering, such as Victor Frankl during his years in Nazi concentration camps. It is a mark of his deep and profound transformative suffering during those years that he could later write in his book, *Man's Search for Meaning*, "It is here that we encounter the central theme of existence: to live is to suffer, to survive is to find meaning in the suffering. For in some ways, suffering ceases to be suffering at the moment it finds a meaning."

Of course, this view also runs into problems of

suffering arising from action not directed by humans. How does human free will explain accidents or natural disasters? Hillsdale College professor Michael Bauman postulates a "divine proclamation" following the first transgression and disobedience by human beings—the Fall of Adam and Eve—which fundamentally alters the way in which the world evolved and operates.

Alternatively, perhaps natural disasters are simply the result of natural geological and environmental factors that largely promote life on this planet. Given either, or perhaps both, of these explanations for natural disasters within our world, it seems possible that considerations of human free will play a role in explaining human suffering.

Thomas Aquinas suggests that even otherwise seemingly meaningless suffering may serve some future purpose but, in the end, God will have victory over suffering.

Regardless of the theoretical and philosophical solutions to the question of suffering, we must encounter people where they are, amid their suffering. It is here that the Christian concept can influence our thinking about human suffering. In the Christian tradition, freedom and love are coexistent: there is no such thing as freedom without love, nor love without freedom. Furthermore, Christianity not only speaks of a God who loved us enough to grant us the necessary freedom to love, but God also manifested true love by becoming incarnate to suffer with humanity.

Now, you might ask, does God really suffer along with the world that he created? In our present time, when the entire world was afflicted by the pandemic, much of our lives took on a different perspective. In view of the impending fear of death and the increasing number of victims, several television programs, radio shows, and social media directives, turned our attention, not to medical professionals or to updated scientists working diligently in their laboratories, but to God, through fervent prayer, and stronger faith and hope.

Soon after our initial scary feelings, our serious protective means, and compulsory isolations, I came across some comforting observations by Father Luke Veronis, a well-known and dedicated Greek Orthodox priest, who had worked many years conducting missions in Africa and Albania. He wrote:

> Suddenly the gasoline went down, pollution went down, people started to have more time—so much time that they do not know what to do with it. Parents are spending time with their kids as a family, work is no longer a priority, nor travel, nor social life. Suddenly, we silently see within ourselves and under-

stand the value of the words "solidarity," "love," "compassion," "strength," "empathy," and "stronger faith."

Sooner than ever, we realized that we are all in the same boat, rich and poor. We see the supermarket shelves empty and the hospitals full and realize how fragile life is. New cars and old cars stand in the garages, simply because nobody can get out.

With emptier streets, we have less pollution, cleaner air, and the land also breathes. Human beings returned to their origins, realizing that with or without money, the important thing is to survive, but to survive together! We are in this together! Today, health is the main thing, even in spite of wanting to have or possess. It took only days for the universe to establish the social equality that was said to be impossible. Fear invaded everyone. Yet we still hope, for nothing can conquer hope. Eventually the evil will be defeated.

These reflections remind us of our venerability as human beings. We are not as invincible and as mighty as we think. Our loving God is in power, and God is with us even during troublesome times. Nature is forcing us to clean up the mess we made and respect God's creation all around us.

The gods in which we invested so much of our time and so much attention—the gods of money, sport, fame, prestige, superiority, and politics—have fallen. The pandemic reminded us of the central aspects of life: our best protection is *God*; our best refuge is *home*; our best company is *family*; and our real time is only *today*. We are not gods. We are not kings. We do not have the power to control anything. We are part of a whole, fragile, brittle, and vulnerable world. We are part of something that we want to dominate; yet through the pandemic our soul, our inner voice, was telling us: stop, appreciate, breathe, respect, and be grateful.

Our loving God does not leave humanity to suffer alone. No, God suffers with us: God wants to "be *with* us," even if suffering is our condition. God, who in Christ-became-man to redeem humanity through the most human experiences—suffering and death—did just that. God is the omnipotent deity. But he is also the Suffering Servant, the God who loved his creation so much that he became human and suffered with his creation. This is the hope, faith, and comfort of the Christian world for all those who are suffering.

The Christian tradition offers a worldview that accounts for both human freedom and divine interaction in the world: freedom which enables us to work to alleviate the suffering of others and divine interaction which gives purpose to our benevolent actions and hope to the world.

Through the framework of a God who suffers with us, we can better understand suffering. This is not to say that there will not be questions and problems surrounding suffering; nor does it mean that suffering will suddenly disappear overnight. But the presence of the Lord Jesus Christ, who joins us in our suffering serves as a great help in combating human suffering and giving hope amid the horror of evil.

There is a totally good and powerful God, ever present among us. But there is also evil in the world. Yes, that evil will eventually be destroyed. Yet the hope of eventual freedom and redemption from suffering cannot lead us to apathy but must call us to action.

While none of the common answers to the question of pain and suffering are entirely satisfactory by themselves, the questions highlight certain concerns which reside in our heart. Our understanding of suffering should enable us to fight against injustice and immorality everywhere.

In his book, *Where the Hell Is God?*, Fr. Richard Leonard reminds us that Easter Sunday is God's response to Good Friday—when life triumphs over death. Now, Jesus did not just come "to die," but *his* death announced the end to *death*. Jesus came to live and to

teach us how to live. Consequently, through his coura-
geous and radical life, and the saving love he embodied
for all humanity, he threatened the political, social, and
religious authorities of his day so much so that they
became the instruments of his execution. However,
God had the last word on Good Friday—Easter Sunday; and on death—life.

Richard Leonard also notes that even though
God is removed from the intricate detail of how things
develop, God is not removed from the drama of our
living, our suffering and dying. God waits patiently for
an invitation to enter our lives at whatever level we
want. Christ meets us where we are, embraces us and
holds us close when the going gets tough, and helps us
find the way forward, and most especially, on that last
day when we find the way home.

༺ ༻

For Reflection

Our faith tells us that God has victory over death and
suffering. In what tangible ways does this victory present itself in your life? When and how have you experienced life amid grief and suffering?

8

Self-Restoration

Self-restoration is a long yet a most rewarding process that can be pursued in two ways. Firstly, we can start from where we are regarding our personal religious orientation or belief system. Our religion or belief system serve our spiritual needs. Depending on one's cultural background a person may consider embarking upon a particular spiritual path. Secondly, we can explore and apply basic human qualities—acceptance and care of others, compassion, forgiveness, goodness, generosity, kindness, and love—what we can call basic spiritual values. Whether you are a believer or a non-believer such behavior is essential. As human beings subjected to similar conditions of life, we all need these basic spiritual values. They facilitate our daily existence and create a more pleasant environment.

Granted, these basic values should be taught and modeled at home early in life, however, it is never too late to reconsider these values today. Being a mature adult endowed with a mental capacity and good intentions, seeking a healthier and happier life, it is good to cultivate these values and integrate them into your daily life.

All major religions can make a good and effective contribution to humanity. Whether divinely inspired or not, they are all designed to make our world a better place and the individual a happier person. However, if any religion is to have an impact on a person, it needs to be embraced and practiced not simply with intellectual or verbal eloquence but with a genuine disposition. For this reason, we respect the diversity of religions and appreciate the spiritual nourishment they offer.

Belonging to a church, a temple, a mosque, or some other form of religious gathering, makes cultivating your basic spiritual values easier and more effective. Involvement in a religious group can create a sense of belonging and of being connected with others. The dynamics of a group interacting and pursuing a common goal, under the genuine guidance of a trained spiritual leader can be most powerful. People who share similar issues and support each other can prove helpful in facing life's adversities with courage, patience, and understanding.

Faith has sustained and supported countless people through difficult times. Sometimes, faith operates in small quiet ways; other times it works through profound transformative experiences. In your personal life, you may have heard or witnessed examples of how faith has helped someone through troubled times.

Personally, I have experienced the power of faith in my own family. Sonia, my twenty-six-year-old niece suffered for much of her life from a disease known as anorexia nervosa, an intense fear of gaining weight and a distorted perception of weight that often equates thinness with self-worth. Her parents took her from one specialist to another without much success. Sonia went from 110 pounds to 68 pounds, a mere skeleton. Drugs, doctors, therapy, and hospitalization proved futile.

Ignoring and refusing to accept any exterior help, Sonia found comfort and relief in her faith. "Our Lord Jesus Christ will make me well," she kept saying, while close relatives and friends were preparing for her funeral. Her parents had no choice but to join their daughter's faith, in prayer and confidence that the Lord Jesus would heal her and restore her health. In her consistent prayers, Sonia's health gradually improved. Her attitude toward life became more positive, and when she regained her total health, she married Anthony, a fine young man whom she had known for years.

Now Sonia is an active and happy mother raising her two children. Through their faith, Sonia and her parents were able to withstand intense hardship for several years. They found comfort and hope in their conviction that God would ultimately reveal his love to them.

We are created with an intense, built-in desire to live life to its fullest—to operate at peak performance. Jesus said, "I came that they may have life, and have it abundantly" (John 10:10). There is a great deal of joy, as we participate in life and living, using what is available to us for our well-being, for our families, and for the good of others.

Many men and women spend years hoping to reach a place and time of peace and quiet in their life. This is called retirement. For some, retirement is a time of boredom and a lack of purpose; for others, it involves getting a monthly income from their financial investments that they have accumulated over the years to provide them with a reasonable lifestyle. Affluence and financial security are two of the most alluring attractions that many people pursue but few attain. Once attained, however, we need to reflect on whether they truly provide a sense of inner peace and joy. Where is God in our life? What importance do we place on our basic spiritual values? Is our financial wealth truly giving us a sense of belonging, and are we living life to the fullest?

As we noted earlier, the Incarnation bridges the gap between God and the world, opening the way for us to be happy and secure in our spiritual life. In becoming man, Christ empowered us to share in his own divine nature. God the Father sent the Holy Spirit into our hearts, to fill us ever more with divine life and power. The apostle Paul urges his followers to put on the mind of Christ (cf. 1 Cor 2:16), so "that you may be strengthened in your inner being with power through his Spirit, and that Christ may dwell in your hearts through faith" (Eph 3:16–17).

Through God's energy and support we not only restore our own selves, but we develop healthier relationships with other people. Love is poured into our hearts through the Holy Spirit (cf. Rom 5:5). It is only through the practice of this unselfish love, that we are in communion with God and with our brothers and sisters. It is through the practice of genuine love that we achieve the purpose of our creation, salvation.

As we interweave the basic spiritual values into our relationships, we participate in God's creative energy. We act on our Lord's behalf, emulating his spirit of compassion, forgiveness, justice, and love; we accept and love those who do not return our love; we find joy and inner peace even in difficult times; we have patience when things are not going as well as we expected; we show kindness toward those who treat us unkindly; and we find strength to resist temptation.

With Christ as our companion—in our work and at home—we can move beyond ambition and success, we can stop worshiping at the false altars of career, prestige, and material things and become restored in Christ. Then our life becomes a contribution to our families, to our church, and to our society. With Christ in our hearts, our world has greater meaning.

Before closing this chapter, I would like to recall an episode of the television program 20/20 with Barbara Walters that I saw some years ago where she asked the multimillionaire Ted Turner, "What is it like to be so wealthy and powerful?" Turner responded, "It is an empty bag!" These stark five words serve as a poignant reminder that, regardless of how much you have attained, it can never be enough. Wealth can never make us feel self-restored. This also reminds me of Jesus's words to the Samaritan woman, "Everyone who drinks of this water will be thirsty again, but those who drink of the water that I will give them will never be thirsty. The water that I will give will become in them a spring of water gushing up to eternal life" (John 4:13–14).

For Reflection

Do you ever feel like your life is like "an empty bag"?
What changes do you think you could make to restore
vitality to your lifestyle and the way you live?

9

Simplicity

The dictionary defines "simplicity" as being direct, clear, free of pretense or dishonesty, free of vanity, and free of complications and distractions. True simplicity is like children at play. They have fun, they think, speak, and act candidly. They believe whatever they are told. When they are with their parents, they cling to them mostly for security and love.

They are not worrying about tomorrow, and they don't think about their past. They take what comes to them in good faith, and enjoy life, simply and without concern for causes and effects. *Dear Lord, help us to observe children as they play and to learn a lesson from their innocent life.*

My aunt, Victoria, was often concerned about the poor and hungry people of our village, Moria in Lesvos, Greece, especially during the Second World

War. Her mental determination was unparalleled as was her will to pass on to me and her two children what she believed. From an early age, we had become vessels into which she poured her knowledge, acquired from her life's experience as a Greek elementary school teacher. I still hear her voice dispensing wisdom and am fortunate to have had that upbringing.

One of the basic messages my aunt implanted in my mind was *pan metron ariston*, which means "moderation in all things." In this exceedingly immoderate age, it rings with a new force as a code to live by when we celebrate family events—birthdays, weddings, anniversaries, graduations, and family successes.

Certainly, these family events ought to be celebrated in a spirit of joy and gratitude. Celebrations can awaken our best feelings among those who are celebrating with us—we are here, we are alive, we are happy, and God has been good to us. In this spirit of joy and friendship it is important to reflect and express our thanks to God and our loved ones. A simple and heartfelt prayer might be: *Lord, fill our lives, our families, and our relationships, with stronger faith, generosity, forgiveness, and love. You know the struggles we have gone through in the past. Lord, let us be as compassionate, forgiving, and loving as you are. Amen.*

When our soul acts, it considers only what it is suitable to do or say, and then acts spontaneously without any thought about what others will think or say. Such thoughts, feelings, and actions of the soul have no other aim than to act in accordance with the will of God, whose existence and presence in our life is pure simplicity.

Christian prudence accompanies the virtue of simplicity and innocence. As Christ said to his disciples, "I am sending you out like sheep into the midst of wolves; so be wise as serpents and innocent as doves" (Matt 10:16). Here, Christ recommends prudence, especially toward the wicked, that they may not be deceived. It is only through simplicity and innocence that God can inspire us with prudence in difficult times or through major obstacles. Consequently, Christ announced to his disciples that the Holy Spirit will inspire them in combatting life's adversities.

The simplicity of God is that of the pure Spirit who is truth and gentleness. In Christ, we are united in the simplest manner the deepest humility and the loftiest dignity. For Christ tells us that he came to serve, not to be served (cf. Matt 20:28).

If you wish to live a life with less stress, consider living more simply. If our life is familiar only with luxurious living, the attempt to simplify your life can be a challenge. To live more simply means to encounter life more directly, fully, and wholeheartedly. When we live with simplicity, we give ourselves and others space to breathe—the gift of less stress and less expectations. Now, to live simply does not mean that we should necessarily abandon all our worldly possessions. However, if we truly seek a sense of equanimity, inner peace, and joy, we need to live with a better balance—not too much and not too little of anything. This will assist our capacity to realize our human potential.

Bringing simplicity into our lives requires that we understand the ways our consumption either supports or hinders our existence. We must learn the difference between those material circumstances that support or restrict our lives. Simplicity requires living with balance. Again, I am reminded of the ancient Greek axiom of my aunt, *pan metron ariston* ("everything in moderation").

Such balance requires an understanding of the difference between our personal "needs" and "wants." Needs are those things that are essential to our survival and growth. Wants are those things that are extra—that gratify our psychological and emotional yearnings and our ambitions. For example, we *need* food and shelter to survive. Healthy and nutritious food is necessary, but does it have to be a fancy six-course meal each time we are hungry? It is a balanced diet that we *need*. We may *want* to eat in expensive restaurants. Does it have to be a high-class restaurant that we cannot afford? We *need* shelter, but does it have to be a huge house with many extra rooms that are seldom used? We *need* basic medical care. We *need* functional clothing. We may *want* designer clothes or frequent changes in clothing style to reflect the latest fashion. We may have to consider the stress that a choice may cause. We *need* transportation. We may *want* a new and fancy Mercedes. But can we afford the repair bills when something goes wrong with it? Perhaps, a good and less expensive car may serve us well and can take us to places with less stress.

Contemporary culture promotes the passion to possess—the good life found in accumulation and the mindset that "more is better." Interestingly, another word for passion is suffering. The lust for affluence in contemporary society has become an epidemic to the extent that we have completely lost touch with reality. Furthermore, the pace of the modern world accentuates our sense of being fractured and fragmented. We feel strained, hurried, breathless, and stressed. The complexity of rushing to achieve a high position or to accumulate more things threatens to overwhelm us; it seems there is no escape from the rat race. We are forced to ask ourselves: What are our choices that cause this excessive stress?

The witness to simplicity is profoundly rooted in the biblical tradition, and most perfectly exemplified in the life of Jesus Christ. When a scribe came to Jesus and said that he was prepared to follow him,

Jesus responded, "Foxes have holes, and birds of the air have nests; but the Son of Man has nowhere to lay his head" (Matt 8:20). In other words, if you want to be a Christian disciple, then this world cannot be your home; you need to simplify your life.

Simplicity is a grace given by God. It is also a discipline, because we are called to do something of essence. Simplicity may not make life simpler, but it does put us in the place where we can receive it. It sets our lives before the life of Christ so that he can work through us and become a model of simplicity.

Christian simplicity is both easy and difficult. It is easy in the same way that all Christian grace works its way into our lives. It is easy in the way that breathing is easy. In simplicity there are times of struggle and effort, times when we despair of our lifestyles and wonder if our life will ever find harmony. But occasionally, in the middle of the struggle, we have a sense of God's presence and grace, and spontaneously we glorify our Father in heaven because we know that we have done no more than receive God's gift. Simplicity is an inward reality that can be seen in an outward lifestyle.

For the Christian, material things are God's created goods for us to enjoy. Consequently, we should not dismiss material things as inconsequential, far worse yet, as evil. The material world is good and meant to make life comfortable. At times, simplicity seems as elusive as humility; the moment we think we have it we have lost it.

I have been fortunate to meet several individuals, couples, and families who live a simple life. These people seem to be happier, more content, exuberant, more empathetic, and more secure because of their simple lifestyles. They seem to have a good self-esteem and are accepting of their own weaknesses.

I once had the good fortune to travel for a month to different parts of Africa with my family. Truly, I witnessed poverty and the lack of many things such as food, clothing, and medicine. But I also experienced a simple yet genuine hospitality, a joyous spirit among many people. They did not need to have many things to be happy. They were conscious of their love of life. I saw their participation in church services, their singing and clapping of hands as their voices were raised high. It seemed that these people were completely connected with God. The melody of their hymns seemed to come from a choir of angels praising God.

Models of simplicity are desperately needed in our times. Our task is urgent and relevant. Our century thirsts for authentic simplicity—enjoying a spirit of prayer, nurturing the soul, and practicing a life of obedience. People who embrace simplicity can hear negative feedback without feeling threatened. They fight less with their partners and are more accommodating and less defensive. As a result, these couples have less stress and more satisfying relationships.

❧ ❦

For Reflection

What makes your life cluttered and complicated? What might you do to simplify your lifestyle today? Is there anyone in your life who is a model of authentic simplicity?

10

Gratitude

This chapter is about being grateful for small things that you may take for granted. It begins by starting each day with a few words: *Thank you God for another day.* Each day, our life is God's gift, but it is our choice to cherish the gift and to say thank you.

Living with gratitude is recognizing the blessings of life whether it is our health, our family and friends, our work, or simply the beauty and glory of nature and our personal pursuits that bring satisfaction. Every year in the month of November we celebrate the day of Thanksgiving in the United States. However, in our everyday life, it is good to be thankful for all encounters—whether we go shopping, meet with a friend, or someone offers us a needed service or opens a door for us. Yet think of a better feeling when we start each day with a few words of gratitude to God for giving us our life.

Major family celebrations also offer a special time, not just to be with our family and loved ones and enjoy a pleasant day and a delicious meal, but to be truly grateful for God's gift of life. It is important to feel grateful for our good health and to belong to a community.

A client, whom we will call Ted, came to me in his late thirties. He was healthy, articulate, and well preserved. His main problem and the reason he sought therapy was that he was experiencing periodical depression and dissatisfaction with his present life. He admitted that he had a good job, a good wife, who also had a great job in a large Wall Street firm in New York. He loved his wife and owned a gorgeous home in Short Hills, New Jersey, and didn't understand why he sometimes felt unhappy and depressed.

"What seems to be missing in your life?" I asked curiously.

"I don't know," he answered.

Now, in my work as a therapist, "I don't know" usually means that a person is hesitating to admit something for fear of appearing weak.

"Is it possible, Ted, that you may lack feelings of gratitude?" I asked.

"Gratitude to whom and for what?" he asked rather annoyed. "I've worked very hard to attain whatever I have; nobody has given me anything."

"What about the things that you take for granted?" I asked.

He paused, and after a brief silence, he asked, "What things?"

In today's fast-paced world, most people don't seem to have time to say, "Thank you, God, for each day." Work, traffic, family, soccer practice for their kids, medical appointments, entertainment, social events, and countless other things become priorities. Many people seem to have no time to be thankful. One wonders why we have so many unhappy people in a country that enjoys plentiful food, shelter, electricity, running water, air conditioning, heating, transportation, sanitation, affluence, and many other blessings.

I looked directly at him, and with a smile said, "Ted, you have eyes that can see, ears that can hear, a brain that can think, hands that can work, feet that can walk. You are alive and healthy. Aren't these givens worthy of some gratitude?"

"Everybody has these," he said, lifting his shoulders to let me know that he was not impressed with my response.

"Well, if you want to be happy, as you get out of bed in the morning, start your day by being grateful for the things that you take for granted. I would like to see you read for a whole week and repeat the following words that come from an anonymous author:

Be thankful that you don't already have
everything you desire.
If you did, what would there be out there
to look forward to?
Be thankful when you don't know
something,
For it gives you the opportunity to learn.
Be thankful for the difficult times.
During those times you grow and get
stronger.
Be thankful for your limitations.
Because they give you opportunities for
improvement.
Be thankful for each new challenge.
Because it will build your strength and
character.

We have so much for which to be thankful. Our realization of what is most important in life goes hand in hand with gratitude for our blessings. *It is always our conscious choice of which secret garden we would like to tend*. When we choose not to focus on what is missing from our lives but are grateful for the abundance that's present—love, health, family, friends, work, the glory of nature, and personal pursuits that bring us happiness even for a little while—the wasteland of illusion falls away and we experience heaven on earth.

Every day is a gift; every breath, every heart pulse, and every step and move that we make is a gift. While it's easy to take these wonderful blessings for granted—and begin to focus on what we *don't* have—millions of people around the world live without these necessities of life. I'll never forget the lack of drinking water that my family and I witnessed on our month's mission in Africa. I remember the words of Bishop Nakiama, when he said, "Some generous person gave me a thousand dollars. I did not know what to do with all that money. So, I spent it drilling a well. Then I saw several men and women traveling two or more kilometers carrying plastic containers which they filled with well water to bring to their homes." The experience made me conscious of the small things in my own life. It is so easy to forget how blessed we are! Maintaining an attitude of gratitude is something we need to reconsider as one of our major goals in life.

> In his proclamation appointing a national day of fast, President Abraham Lincoln stated,

"We have been the recipients of the choicest bounties of Heaven. We have been preserved, these many years, in peace and prosperity. We have grown in numbers, wealth and power, as no other nation has ever grown. But we have forgotten God. We have forgotten the gracious hand which preserved us in peace, and multiplied and enriched and strengthened us; and we have vainly imagined, in the deceitfulness of our hearts, that all these blessings were produced by some superior wisdom and virtue of our own."[1]

This is a tremendously powerful statement! Since the time that President Lincoln gave this speech, the wealth, prosperity, and peace experienced by the United States is far greater—as is also the attitude of pride, selfishness, and ingratitude. But if this same speech were given today, there would be an uproar! In contrast to the time of Lincoln's message, or even fifty years ago, today's attitude of ingratitude is far worse. If that generation *forgot* God and the many blessings bestowed on America, then this generation doesn't even know God exists!

1. Abraham Lincoln, "Proclamation Appointing a National Fast Day," March 30, 1863, Washington, DC, www.abrahamlincolnonline.org.

In this world of being obsessed with what's "in"—the newest fashions, the latest songs, and the absurd political correctness—gratitude has almost been declared unconstitutional.

᪥ ᪥

For Reflection

For what are you most grateful for in your life today? Try beginning each day with a prayer of gratitude for your life and blessings.

11

Kindness

The fifth fruit of the Holy Spirit is kindness, which is taught to us in the New Testament: "Let all bitterness and wrath and anger and clamor and slander be put away from you, with all malice, and be kind to one another, tenderhearted, forgiving one another, as God in Christ forgave you" (Eph 4:31–32). As we think seriously about kindness, we realize its uniqueness and how it enriches the other gifts and fruits of the Holy Spirit making our life more effective.

Unfortunately, some people go through much of their life without experiencing acts of kindness. Indeed, many people are psychologically confused, wounded, and scarred by being neglected or rejected. Furthermore, depression, fear, anger, negativity, and suspicion hinder many acts of kindness.

In the Book of Proverbs, we read that "a soft tongue will break a bone" (Prov 25:15). In other words, no one can overcome the power of gentleness with evil. Gentleness, kindness, and meekness, make heavenly things appear exceedingly great and the earthly things almost inanimate.

The apostle Paul offers us a strong message: "But we were gentle among you, like a nurse taking care of her children. So, being affectionately desirous of you, we were ready to share with you not only the gospel of God but also our own selves, because you had become very dear to us" (1 Thess 2:7–8). Through Paul's kindness, his care and goodness, everything that was hard was crushed so that the church could grow up in genuine brotherly love as children of the light, waiting for Jesus Christ's return.

Today, with the various pressures of work and society, many people have lost the ability to treat others with kindness and respect. Consequently, more people who need support grow impatient. In contrast, St. Paul teaches us the extraordinary gift of God's goodness and kindness.

The quality of kindness goes hand in hand with the quality of love. Through the love of the Holy Spirit, the quality of kindness follows on from it. In other words, once the love of God flows more into your personal life, you cannot help but be more kind to others as do many of the other fruits of the Holy Spirit. Essentially, human beings have the potential to care. When we learn to respect the image and likeness of God in ourselves and in others, we will then be kind to ourselves and to others.

Kindness requires patience. By practicing kindness, we will start to see others differently; we will understand others with a capacity to be kind despite some outwardly unloving behaviors. But, why bother? Because we live together in a world where our own peace of mind and the health of our body and soul are totally dependent on our relationships with others.

Of course, if someone in your path treats you badly or blocks your growth with negative thoughts, try to understand that these people project on you their own mental conditions. At best you can avoid them. A saying that has often been attributed to Eleanor Roosevelt is worth recalling here: "No one can make you feel inferior without your consent."

It is important to think about how we deal with everyday people we encounter: family members, the mail carrier, the janitor, the garbage collector, the dentist, or the cashier at the supermarket. How do you relate to these various people?

Jesus Christ practiced radical kindness. He always had great compassion for both women and men, for children and adults, for both Jews and Gentiles, for the sick and the strong.

As we look at the people around us, we, too, should be moved with compassion. We, too, should strive to be merciful and compassionate—in other words, we should strive to be kind to each other.

When we consider the life of Jesus in the New Testament, we can see that in his dealings with others, Jesus emphasized that we must be kind to everyone, not just friends and family, "You have heard that it was said, 'You shall love your neighbor and hate your enemy.' But I say to you, Love your enemies and pray for those who persecute you" (Matt 5:43–44) and "Do to others as you would have them do to you. If you love those who love you, what credit is that to you? For even sinners love those who love them" (Luke 6:31–34).

I would like to conclude this chapter with the moving story of Shay, a student at a school that serves children with learning disabilities, that was told at a fundraising dinner. The following speech will be remembered by all who attended.

> I believe that when a child like Shay, who was mentally and physically disabled comes into the world, an opportunity to realize true human nature presents itself, and it comes in the way other people treat that child.

Shay and I had walked past a park where some boys Shay knew were playing baseball. Shay asked, "Do you think they'll let me play?" I knew that most of the boys would not want someone like Shay on their team, but as a father I also understood that if my son were allowed to play, it would give him a much-needed sense of belonging and some confidence to be accepted by others in spite of his handicaps.

I approached one of the boys on the field and asked (not expecting much) if Shay could play. The boy looked around for guidance and said, "We're losing by six runs and the game is in the eighth inning. I guess he can be on our team, and we'll try to put him in to bat in the ninth inning."

Shay struggled over to the team's bench and, with a broad smile, put on a team shirt. I watched with a small tear in my eye and warmth in my heart. The boys saw my joy at my son being accepted. In the bottom of the eighth inning, Shay's team scored a few runs but was still behind by three. In the top of the ninth inning, Shay put on a glove and played in the right field. Even though no hits came his way, he was obviously ecstatic just to be in the game and on the field, grinning from ear to ear as I waved to him from the stands. In the bottom of the ninth inning, Shay's team scored again. Now, with two outs and the bases loaded, the potential winning run was on base, and Shay was scheduled to be next at bat.

At this juncture, do they let Shay bat and give away their chance to win the game? Surprisingly, Shay was given the bat. Everyone knew that a hit was all but impossible because Shay didn't even know how to hold the bat properly, much less connect with the ball.

However, as Shay stepped up to the plate, the pitcher, recognizing that the other team was putting winning aside for this moment in Shay's life, moved in a few steps to lob the ball in softly so Shay could at least make contact. The first pitch came, and Shay swung clumsily and missed. The pitcher again took a few steps forward to toss the ball softly toward Shay. As the pitch came in, Shay swung at the ball and hit a slow ground ball right back to the pitcher.

The game would now be over. The

pitcher picked up the soft grounder and could have easily thrown the ball to the first baseman. Shay would have been out and that would have been the end of the game.

Instead, the pitcher threw the ball right over the first baseman's head, out of reach of all teammates. Everyone from the stands and both teams started yelling, "Shay, run to first! Never in his life had Shay ever run that far, but he made it to first base. He scampered down the baseline, wide-eyed and startled.

Everyone yelled, "Run to second, run to second!" Catching his breath, Shay awkwardly ran toward second, gleaming and struggling to make it to the base. By the time Shay rounded toward second base, the right fielder had the ball. The smallest guy on their team who now had his first chance to be the hero for his team. He could have thrown the ball to the second-baseman for the tag, but he understood the pitcher's intentions so he, too, intentionally threw the ball high and far over the third-baseman's head. Shay ran toward third base deliriously as the runners ahead of him circled the bases toward home.

All were screaming, "Shay, Shay, Shay, all the way, Shay!"

Shay reached third base because the opposing shortstop ran to help him by turning him in the direction of third base, and shouted, "Run to third!"

As Shay rounded third, the boys from both teams, and the spectators, were on their feet screaming, "Shay, run home! Run home!" Shay ran to home, stepped on the plate, and was cheered as the hero who hit the grand slam and won the game for his team.

That day, said the father softly with tears now rolling down his face, the boys from both teams helped bring a piece of true love and humanity into this world.

Shay didn't make it to another summer. He died that winter, having never forgotten being the hero and making his father so happy, and coming home and seeing his mother tearfully embrace her little hero of the day! ("All The Way Shay!" author unknown)

We have thousands of opportunities every single day to help realize the "natural order of things," and this story of Shay highlights the choice that we are often faced with in our interactions with people: Do we pass along a spark of love and humanity, or do we pass up those opportunities and leave the world a little bit colder in the process? The boy who chose to let Shay play on the team impacted the rest of the game and made all of the players heroes.

A famous quote from Mahatma Gandhi springs to mind here: "The true measure of any society can be found in how it treats its most vulnerable members."

જ઼ જ઼

For Reflection

How did the story of Shay inspire you? What are some of the examples and opportunities in your life to pass along a spark of love and humanity?

12

Our Human Potential

A sign of maturity is recognizing our human potential. Our true self-worth comes from knowing our human potential, the lifelong yearning of our soul, our inner self.

When we discover our incredible human potential, we feel a sense of maturity as we strive to live up to it, and as our life blossoms and bears rewarding results.

To discover our human potential, the real meaning and purpose of our life, we need to ask ourselves a few simple questions: Am I happy that today is another day in my life? Are my activities lifegiving or routine? Am I doing things that are important to myself and of benefit to others?

For myself, life has been a journey that began when I was a village teenager, an ordinary olive picker, in Greece. I picked up olives to cure, to eat, and hopefully sell. Twice a week, I grazed our goats that provided milk for our family. It was during this time that Hitler invaded Greece. I hated the Nazis. Their cruelty and intimidation caused fear. Food and bread became scarce, and people died of starvation. The invasion lasted almost four years. But when the Nazis eventually left, the communists took over, destroying the ruins the Nazis left behind.

I was fortunate that, during World War II, the United States government extended an invitation to all American citizens, who were living overseas, to return to their homeland. By birth, I was born in Philadelphia, and so, as a citizen, I was able to return to America. Six months after my arrival, I went to a seminary at Brookline, Massachusetts, to study theology. I then took courses in pastoral counseling at Philadelphia Divinity School. Upon graduation, I became a priest in the Greek Orthodox Church. Then, after more than twenty years, I sensed an increasing desire to pursue missionary work.

During my years of ministry, I was able to initiate and coordinate an open-heart surgery mission to Athens, Greece. At that time, such surgery was not available in Greece, and patients who needed it had to go to Italy, England, or America.

In 1967, ladies from our church helped to bring

three young boys from Greece to St. Vincent's Hospital in Los Angeles, California. These boys suffered from heart failure and needed surgery. Unfortunately, two of them did not survive.

The sadness of their loss propelled me to pursue my plans of bringing a team of doctors from America to Greece. Through the courtesy of the heart surgeons of Loma Linda University Hospital of California, the support from Jacqueline Kennedy Onassis, and years of diligent work, over a thousand surgeries were performed between the years 1968 to 1974.

But there were crazy obstacles to overcome: Who is this priest who wants to bring American doctors to Greece? We don't need foreign aid. We have our own competent doctors. Besides, we are not an undeveloped country!

The Greek military government began to investigate me. The local doctors in Greece did not want doctors coming from the United States. Their negative response and suspicions went rampant. Even my archbishop advised me not to be involved with doctors and hospitals but to be mindful of my spiritual duties as a parish priest.

It was extremely frustrating. I had a record of eight hundred names, young and older Greek patients who needed heart surgery within the next two years. After a few sleepless nights, I woke up one day feeling a vitality, an energy, within me that needed to be translated into action. I could not stop now!

After the first successful mission, I called Dr. Ellsworth Wareham at the Loma Linda University Hospital of California and requested his help for a second mission for those heart patients in Greece who needed surgery. Fortunately, the president of the hospital approved a second missionary effort to Athens, Greece.

The three strongest sources of support were *prayer*, *persistence*, and *patience*. Finally, by God's grace, the Onassis Cardiovascular Center in Athens was eventually established. Today, this Center performs approximately two thousand surgeries a year.

At the end of this heart mission to Greece, I went through years of intense training and became a psychotherapist, as well as a part-time professor, teaching courses in psychology at the graduate school of Seaton Hall University in New Jersey. Yet my missionary passion continued during the summer of 1977 and carried me and my family to both Kenya and Uganda in Africa. There we experienced the spirit of hope, faith, and medicine with the indigenous, and provided donations to drill seven wells for much-needed drinking water in Uganda.

Beyond our human distractions and superficial behavior and interaction with others, we are people with great potential. We need to respect the image and likeness of God in ourselves and in others and to be kind to ourselves and to others. This is an important key in discovering our inner potential and purpose in life. For when we fully understand our purpose in life, we experience joy, satisfaction, excitement, energy, passion, and self-expression.

If you are lost somewhere between your family obligations, life challenges, and your job, consider this olive picker's adventurous journey. Consider the much deeper meaning of your life as you grow and become aware of your inner potential. This is the road to maturity and the way to build a better world. Hopefully, these examples of my journey in life will help you to consider your own potential. It is by tapping into our human potential that we can and will develop a more defined purpose in our life. It begins by imagining yourself becoming a better and more satisfied person with your life.

༈ ༈

For Reflection

To discover your human potential, ask yourself: Are you happy that today is another day in your life? Are your activities lifegiving or routine? Are you doing things that are important to you and of benefit to others?

Epilogue

Hopefully, in reading this book, you have learned a great deal about yourself—your strengths, weaknesses, and emotional issues. In becoming more familiar with yourself, you can embrace who you are and not be simply the person whom others may want you to be. As you look into the mirror, you can appreciate that you are a son or a daughter of a loving God. Cherish that feeling of acceptance and respect for yourself.

Self-respect is about finding a deep sense of self-worth and self-love and acknowledging that you are just as worthy of receiving love as you are to love. Knowing that God both loves and respects you form the very foundation of self-respect and of finding our true purpose in life. After all, God knows all about you and continues to love you.

If you have a sense of who you really are—the true person—then you know the importance of giving

yourself honor and respect. In this regard, it is important to take good care of your body, mind, and soul every
day. This is the greatest gift that our Creator has given
us. Diligent self-care keeps us healthy, fit, resilient, and
content. Practicing self-care can be a challenge since
many of us tend to be very busy and have responsibilities at work and at home. As we noted in the earlier
chapters of this book, our work and responsibilities can
lead to stress. Stress generally refers to two things: psychological pressure that stems from real or perceived
demands imposed on one person by another individual, group, or environment; and the body's response
to it that involves multiple systems, from digestion to
metabolism to muscles tightness and even some memory loss.

When you take time out, specifically to rest, relax,
or have fun, try not to feel guilty. Self-respect does *not*
create a problem unless we go about it the wrong way.
Remember that the self-respect we crave comes from
within us and that external factors usually offer tempo-
rary happiness.

Firstly, consider ways to respect yourself properly.
Become more aware of your needs by honoring your
commitments or promises to others. But be sure to
consider what the commitment involves before agree-
ing to it. In doing this, we are not only respecting our
own limitations, but also being honest with ourselves

and the other person. Responding with honesty is not only less work but it is more enjoyable.

Secondly, consider the tasks that motivate your passion and excite you. My wife and I became interested in missionary work. Through our church, we were given an opportunity to experience the faith and vitality of the indigenous people of Kenya and Uganda. This venture excited all members of our family, as we discovered that we received so much more from these people than we could ever bring to Africa. Many people have good intentions, but their personal life is often clouded by their personal needs. You may be surprised when you rediscover your own capacity to love.

Thirdly, each day, love those who are close to you—your family, your friends, and colleagues. Many people are soothed and healed by the tenderness of love. Then return to your inner self, your soul, and realize that everything in this world has a purpose.

Finally, as you explore your inner resources, you will discover that you have more potential than you can possibly imagine. If you feel even for a moment that your personal life has no purpose, this is your moment to create one. Nobody else will do it for you. This is your human task and your choice.